Cambridge
in old picture postcards

by
Michael Rouse

European Library - Zaltbommel/Netherlands MCMLXXXIV

GB ISBN 90 288 2960 1 / CIP

European Library in Zaltbommel/Netherlands publishes among other things the following series:

IN OLD PICTURE POSTCARDS *is a series of books which sets out to show what a particular place looked like and what life was like in Victorian and Edwardian times. A book about virtually every town in the United Kingdom is to be published in this series. By the end of this year about 175 different volumes will have appeared. 1,250 books have already been published devoted to the Netherlands with the title* **In oude ansichten.** *In Germany, Austria and Switzerland 500, 60 and 15 books have been published as* **In alten Ansichten;** *in France by the name* **En cartes postales anciennes** *and in Belgium as* **En cartes postales anciennes** *and/or* **In oude prentkaarten** *150 respectively 400 volumes have been published.*

For further particulars about published or forthcoming books, apply to your bookseller or direct to the publisher.

This edition has been printed and bound by Grafisch Bedrijf De Steigerpoort in Zaltbommel/Netherlands.

INTRODUCTION

Cambridge is perhaps one of the best known towns in the world because of its ancient University. In 1951 Cambridge officially became a city and today has a population of some 100,000 and as well as the University has a growing reputation as a centre for the modern technological industries, many of them linked with the University. It is also, of course, a centre for shopping and recreation.

During the period of the earliest photographs in this book the population was about 40,000 and by the 1930's with the addition of parts of Chesterton, Cherry Hinton and Trumpington Cambridge had grown geographically and from a population count to about 60,000.

During this century the hold of the University on the town — powerful enough to force the railway right on to the edge of the town in the 1840's and to stop trams running on Sundays and to have its own gaol in the Spinning House — was being loosened. The railway brought large areas of working men's housing in the Romsey Town and Mill Road part, while after the First World War large areas of council houses spread the town even further.

It would have been easy, but very dull, to have filled the pages of this book with photographs of the Colleges. There are many hundred and any dealer would be delighted to sell them at modest prices, but they do not reflect the changing face of Cambridge. I have, therefore, looked for postcards that do show the changing face of Cambridge and preferably ones that have not been reproduced time and again.

In this search my thanks go to Alan Fordham, of the Granta Stamp and Coin shop in Magdalene Street, and Bill Kirkland, of London, for the loan of cards from their private collections. My gratitude also to Michael Petty, A.L.A. for steering me so expertly around the Cambridgeshire Collection at the Central Library in Cambridge and for the opportunity to select photographs from their vast resources.

The Cambridgeshire Collection has many negatives and prints of the photographic postcards of Ted Mott. Mr. K.P. Humphries of Milton also has a collection of his photographs, prints of which are also in the Cambridgeshire Collection. I am grateful to Mr. Humphries both for information about Ted Mott, summarised briefly elsewhere, and for permission to reproduce some of these photographs. Ted Mott was a fine photographer recording Cambridge in the 1920's and really merits a book to himself, perhaps this book might stimulate such a publication.

In researching the captions for the photographs, particular thanks again to Michael Petty and Chris Jakes, A.L.A. and the staff of the Cambridgeshire Collection. Several books have proved particularly useful, especially Sara Payne's 'Down Your Street' volume 1, which gives a fascinating word and picture portrait of the streets of central Cambridge. There are the various works of F.A. Reeve, especially 'Victorian and Edwardian Cambridge from old photographs' and the late Enid Porter's marvellous fund of information 'Cambridgeshire Customs and Folklore'. The Oleander Press of Cambridge has published many entertaining and informative booklets on the City and for further study of some of the subjects touched upon in this book I can recommend 'Cam Bridges' by Richard J. Pierpoint, 'Cambridge Buses' by Mark Seal and 'Varsity Rags and Hoaxes' by F.A. Reeve. For background reading on the picture postcard publishers in the county 'Cambridgeshire in Early Postcards' is also still available from the Oleander Press and Bookshops. 'Rowing on the Cam' by James Douglas (Birds Farm Publications) I found most useful and 'Trams in Cambridge' by Nigel Pennick (Electric Traction Publications) gives a detailed history of the trams which this book merely touches. My thanks also go to that remarkable Cambridge author and remarkable man, Jack Overhill, for his help.

To Dan Jackson of the 'Cambridge Evening News', my thanks for his assistance in trying to find information about some elusive cards. My particular thanks to Miss Jean Robson, Mr. Richard Naylor and Mr. Bernhard Matthew for supplying information as a result of a 'Cambridge Evenings News' appeal through their 'Looking Back' feature. Also to the 'Cambridge Evening News' my gratitude for being allowed to reproduce the final illustration in the book.

I make no apology for including the cartoon cards of Harry Moden and Frank Keene, for they have great charm and wit and they do depict many aspects of Cambridge life, especially where the University and the town met.

This book is not a comprehensive history, more a pictorial scrapbook or kaleidoscope — past streets, shops, faces frozen in time, University customs, royal visits, the river, the First World War, trams and early buses. It is not meant to be a mournful procession, for the City lives and changes and not all change is for the worse.

Finally my thanks go to the photographers. Where they are known, like William Tams and Ted Mott, they are named. Many, however, were the anonymous employees of national postcard companies like the Kingsway Real Photo Company. Whoever they were their work exists, albeit it has to be found, and it helps us to see again and understand the Cambridge of one hundred to fifty years ago.

1. The photographer sets up his camera on Market Hill looking across the front of the canopied Guildhall into Petty Cury. He records the bustle of carts and people as they crowd the street alongside the market stalls. The year must be about 1890. Today, less than one hundred years on, not one building that can be seen survives.

2. The new Market Place was laid out in 1853 following a disastrous fire which had broken out on the night of Saturday 15th September 1849. The old market had occupied the eastern side of the present Market Hill and then ran in an L-shape between Petty Cury and Peas Hill. The buildings lost in the fire and the subsequent demolition of others made the open space that is known today. In 1855 a fountain was built with gothic style superstructure. Hobson's Conduit, which brought fresh water from Nine Wells, Trumpington, into Cambridge, had stood on the Market Hill from 1614, but it was removed in 1855 to the corner of Trumpington Road and Lensfield Road. This photograph would appear to date from the 1890's.

Market Hill, Cambridge.

3. This later view of the Market Hill shows the original site of the Victoria Cinema. The Victoria Assembly Rooms were built in 1897 and became the Electric Theatre Picture House in 1911. In 1915, after refurbishment, they reopened as the Victoria Cinema and it stayed on that site until 1929. A new Victoria Cinema opened in 1931 on a site nearer the corner of Market Street. The first premises occupied by Boots the Chemist when they came to Cambridge in the 1890's, can also be seen. The railings around the underground toilets which were opened in 1900 can also be seen quite clearly. The photograph probably dates from around 1916.

4. This aerial view was taken from the spire of Holy Trinity Church about 1890 looking towards Great St. Mary's Church. King's College Chapel and other College buildings can be seen in the distance. The market is now fully set out and on the far side of the Market Place at the east end of the church a row of horse-drawn taxi-cabs patiently await customers as do their modern equivalent today at the same point.

5. A view of the Market Hill again showing Great St. Mary's Church, this time it is in the years just after the placing of the memorial to the men of the Cambridgeshire Regiment who fell in the Boer War. Lord Methuen unveiled the memorial on 12th June 1905. The gothic top of the fountain rises above the surrounding stalls, as it continued to do until 1953 when it was found to be unsafe and was removed to the yard of the Folk Museum.

6. In the 1920's the Peas Hill Cash Drapery Stores, G.H. Lavender proprietor, stood on the corner of St. Edmund's Passage. W. & R. Fletcher, family butcher, was at No. 2, while Shrive & Son, basket makers, were at No. 3, with Sydney Parish, chemist, next to that. For centuries Peas Hill had been the site of a fish market and indeed when Maynard Keynes built the Arts Theatre on land behind Peas Hill, with a narrow entrance passage way coming out next to these premises, he suggested calling it the Fish Market Theatre.

7. The 'White Swan' public house, selling Beales Noted Ales and Stout, is photographed here around 1892. The 'White Swan' was one of several public houses in Petty Cury. It stood on the north side. By 1901 the premises had been incorporated into Hallack and Bond's grocery store which occupied nos. 36 to 41 Petty Cury until 1926. Patrick Beale and Co, corn merchants and maltsters, was one of Cambridge's many small breweries in Victorian times.

PETTY CURY, CAMBRIDGE.

8. Petty Cury, or the 'Little Cookery', was one of the best known and busiest streets in the town. Situated just off the Market Hill, here were some of the town's major inns: the 'Lion', 'Falcon', 'Red Hart', 'The Wrestlers', the 'Coach and Horses', 'The Star and Garter', as well as 'The White Swan'. 'The Wrestlers Inn', reputed to be one of the finest buildings in the city, was demolished and the site used for the new Post Office which opened in December 1885 and can be seen in the left foreground of this view which looks westward and dates from around the time of the First World War.

S 1923   PETTY CURY, CAMBRIDGE

9. Postally used in 1912 this photograph taken a little further down the street captures the character of Petty Cury with its collection of popular shops. Alexandra House can be seen on the left of the photograph. At this time Heffer's Bookshop was in Petty Cury and had been since 1896, not far away on the south side was the 'Lion' later to give its name the controversial Lion Yard redevelopment in the 1970's. The Lion Yard shopping precinct replaced the whole of the northern side of Petty Cury and covered the area of little streets and yards behind it.

10. Sidney Street underwent huge changes in the period between the wars with the major stores vying for position. Here is the eastern side seen from Holy Trinity Church. Many small shops were lost when Marks and Spencer and Woolworth built huge stores here in the early 1930's. This was taken about 1890 at the same time as photograph no. 4.

11. On the western side many small shops were lost when Boots, who had opened a branch in Petty Cury some years before, extended their store in an L-shape and opened a new and more impressive entrance onto Sidney Street in 1929. A plaque on the present store records that Charles Darwin had a tenancy there in 1828 when he was at Christ's College.

12. Nearby the corner of Hobson Street and Sussex Street was demolished with most of Sussex Street to form a new shopping crescent. This photograph appears to have been taken shortly before the clearance of the old properties.

SIDNEY STREET, CAMBRIDGE

S 1922

13. The corner of Galloway and Porter's bookshop can be seen in the right foreground next to Sidney Sussex College. Sidney Sussex was built on the site of a thirteenth century Franciscan Friary in the late sixteenth century. Oliver Cromwell, one time Lord Protector of England, became a fellow commoner at the college in 1616. Galloway and Porter's well known new and antiquarian bookshop was established in Sidney Street in 1902. At the time of this Edwardian photograph John Johnson, tailor and clothier, and Frederick Moore, tobacconist, were opposite.

14. The top of Holy Sepulchre, the famous Norman round church in Bridge Street, can be seen over the trees, now gone, in this turn of the century photograph. There is also a tantalising glimpse of Round Church Street where it forks down Ram Yard. At the place where the roads forked stood at this time Prziborsky's barber's shop. The shop with other buildings was later cleared in 1961 to widen the street which is now the entrance to the Park Street multi-story car park. In this study of more leisurely times the young ladies with their bicycles talk in the roadway while the road sweeper, broom in hand, contemplated the progress of the horse-drawn cart from St. John's Street.

15. The George Commercial Hotel stood in Round Church Street behind the church itself as can be seen from the corner of the church yard. The corner of the barber's shop can be seen on the left and narrowness of Round Church Street can be judged. The George Hotel was demolished in 1884 so that a north wing extension could be added to the Union Society building which had been built behind the Round Church in 1866.

Bridge Street, Cambridge.

16. One of the best postcard photographers in the early years of this century in Cambridge was William Tams. He was butler to a master of St. John's College and a keen amateur photographer. Later he became a professional photographer and official photographer to the University. Here he was in Bridge Street, near the Round Church, looking towards Magdalene Street. The buildings on the left were demolished by St. John's College to make space for their Music School in 1938. On the right of the view on the corner of Thompson's Lane is Norman Bradley, the pawnbroker. The traditional pawnbroker's sign of three balls can be clearly seen on the corner of the building.

MAGDALENE COLLEGE, CAMBRIDGE.

17. Magdalene College from the cast iron bridge built in 1823 and designed by Arthur Browne. This was always the principal crossing point over the Cam into the city. A succession of wooden bridges was replaced by a stone bridge designed by local architect James Essex in 1754. When the stone bridge was declared to be 'in decay and ruinous' in 1799 money was raised for the iron bridge which was of a revolutionary design with a three-pin arch. Because of its importance in recent years it has been strengthened rather than replaced by a new bridge.

Old Houses at Bullen's, Cambridge

18. Bullen's Boatyard and Fisher Lane are here seen from Magdalene Bridge. Fisher Lane was a small wharf demolished in 1932 by Magdalene College. It was the last of the small wharves on the river surviving from the middle ages. Others like Flax Hythe, Corn Hythe and Salt Hythe took their names from the goods landed there. In the photograph, postally used in 1928 but looking much earlier about 1905, can be seen on the left an early garden punt. The pleasure punts so associated with this stretch of the Cam first made their appearance in Cambridge around 1902-1904.

S 12556   MAGDALEN COLLEGE, CAMBRIDGE.

19. Magdalene College, and not the spelling on this Edwardian card which is how it is spelt at the 'other place', was founded by Thomas, Baron Audley, in 1542 on the site of an ancient Benedictine Priory, which had become Buckingham College in 1483. Distinguished graduates from Magdalene include Samuel Pepys and he paid for the building of the Pepys' Library in the seventeenth century, and Charles Kingsley, the Victorian author. The attractive ancient street frontage which gives Magdalene Street so much of its charm and historic interest can just be seen opposite the College.

Castle Street, Cambridge.

20. The cross roads where Magdalene Street runs into Castle Street, Chesterton Lane comes in from the right and meets Northampton Street. 'Ye Olde White Horse' was a sixteenth century inn until 1934 when it became the Cambridge and County Folk Museum housing a priceless collection of domestic and rural bygones. This photograph was taken by Ted Mott and shows the junction before the traffic lights. It is a companion photograph to a view of Northampton Street with even the same policeman on point duty.

21. A view of Castle Street taken from opposite the Folk Museum and looking up the hill. Spencer Howe's draper's shop can be seen in the left foreground. The photograph like the previous one dates from the 1920's.

22. This impressive County Court building stood on Castle Street, where the front car park for Shire Hall is now. Described in the 1904 Kelly's Directory as 'a structure of brick and stone in the Italian style, with a portico supported on columns; the interior comprises two courts with grand jury and magistrates' rooms and the usual offices... The assizes for the county, the Isle of Ely and Huntingdonshire and sessions for the county are held here'. The building was demolished in 1954 and within recent years new Magistrates' Courts have been built on top of the Lion Yard multi-story car park.

23. His Majesty's prison and House of Correction was built around 1802 on the Castle Hill. The old castle that once stood on the hill had been used as a prison before that. The building ceased to be used as a prison in 1916, but was not finally demolished until 1931, at the time the new Shire Hall was built on Castle Hill.

Chesterton Lane, Cambridge.

24. Another William Tams photograph dating from about 1896 but postally used in 1907. The cottages on the left hand side were demolished in 1911. W. Collin's woodyard can be seen at the junction of Chesterton Lane with Northampton Street. The woodyard adjoined the 'White Horse Inn' until removed in 1911, presumably to widen the road at that point.

Northampton Street Corner, Cambridge.

25. This Ted Mott photograph, the companion to the Castle Street view, but this time showing the back view of the policeman, also shows the change in the Chesterton Lane corner brought about by the earlier demolition of the cottages and their replacement by a high wall. With the woodyard also gone the road is now quite wide. The newsagents on the corner adjoins an attractive range of eighteenth century or earlier dwellings which were renovated by Magdalene College in 1966.

26. Merchant's General and Provision Stores stood in Northampton Street on the corner of Kettles Yard. The spire of St. Peter's Church on Castle Hill can be seen. The late seventeenth century 'Spotted Cow' was a public house until 1921 eventually becoming part of the clearance that allowed the Honey Hill cottages to be built. In this 1920's photograph one of the errand boys' delivery bicycles, once such a feature of the street scene, belonged to Metcalfe's, the stationers, of Trinity Street.

27. Northampton Street was formerly called Bell Lane, taking its name from the Bell Inn. After 1912 the Bell Inn ceased to be a public house and the time of this photograph, around 1930, was the premises of A. Clark, motor and cycle agent, with the old inn yard used as a garage.

ST. ANDREW'S ST., CAMBRIDGE.

28. The narrowness of St. Andrew's Street is illustrated by this card postally used in 1923 and looking towards the point where Sidney Street and Hobson Street join it. On the right is the First Court of Christ's College, completed by Lady Margaret Beaufort, the mother of Henry VII. At one time the thirteenth century Barnwell Gate stood at this point, one of the fortifications erected by Henry III during his troubles with the rebellious barons. Part of the Great St. Andrew's Church can be seen in the left foreground and the spire of Lloyds Bank can be seen in the distance.

29. Robert Sayle's store still dominates this section of St. Andrew's Street today as it did in this view of some seventy years ago. Robert Sayle opened his drapery business on the site in 1840. In Victorian times many of the shop's employees lived in a hostel on the upper floors of the store. Shop hours were long and the hostel strictly controlled. Men had to be in by 10 p.m., although an half hour extension was granted once a week for courting. The girls had to be in by 9 p.m.

30. 'Ye Olde Castel Hotel' in St. Andrew's Street, was of of the city's leading hotels. Here was the terminus for the London to Cambridge coaches. The hotel was destroyed by fire in 1927 and part of the site was used to build 'The Castle' public house soon afterwards, while in 1937 the Regal Cinema was built on the rest of the site. The Regal is now a two screen cinema renamed the ABC 1 and 2. The spire that can be seen on the Baptist Chapel was removed during the Second World War.

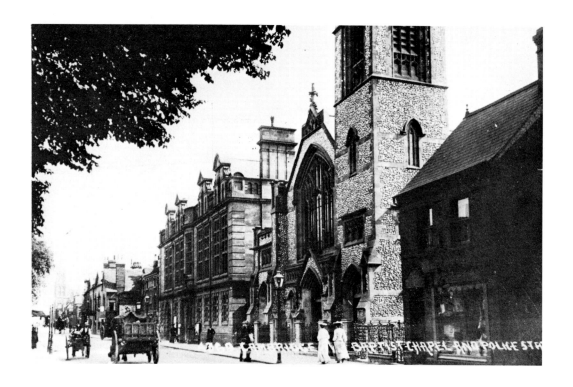

31. The photographer here has moved a little further along St. Andrew's Street and now focuses upon the Baptist Chapel and the Police Station. While a Baptist Chapel was established near the site in the early eighteenth century, the present building was opened in 1904. The Police Station built in 1901 was constructed on the site of the Spinning House. Since the building of a new Police Station at Parkside, the old Police Station has been used by the City Council for its Housing Department.

32. This is the Spinning House which formerly stood on the site where the Police Station was built. It was founded in 1628 by Thomas Hobson, the famous Cambridge carrier who has gone to immortality in the phrase Hobson's choice, which amounts to no choice at all. That was connected with his method of hiring out horses, not the Spinning House which was a place of correction and poor house. Here the inmates were put to work spinning. During the last century it became almost entirely a prison for prostitutes convicted by the University Vice-Chancellor's court. Eventually at the end of the century the much-hated Spinning House was given up by the University and demolished.

33. Looking back up St. Andrew's Street this photograph gives a different view of the 'Olde Castel Hotel'. Next to it can be seen the Belfast Linen warehouse first opened in Regent Street in 1905, but moved in 1908 to the position seen here and the one it occupies today.

34. The University Arms on Regent Street was opened in May 1834 by W. Bird. The hotel enjoyed a superb aspect overlooking Parker's Piece. In the early 1920's the Bradford family bought the freehold of the hotel from Jesus College and extensively enlarged it in 1925. On the left of this Edwardian photograph can be seen the steel framework of the hotel's large garage.

REGENT ST., CAMBRIDGE.

35. A view of Regent Street in the 1920's, the card was postally used in 1927, looking towards the Catholic Church.

36. The tall town houses of Park Terrace, built between 1831 and 1835, seen from Parker's Piece. They look little changed externally today.

S 12563   PARKERS PIECE, CAMBRIDGE.

37. Parker's Piece is possibly one of the best known grass open spaces in the country. The name is synonymous with countless games of cricket, football and hockey. The great Sir Jack Hobbs played cricket on Parker's Piece before finding fame with Surrey and the M.C.C. A pavilion, now used as a restaurant, was built to commemorate his name in 1930 and his playing record was displayed on boards inside. On 28th June 1838 some 14,000 poor men and women and children celebrated the Coronation of Queen Victoria with a meal on the Piece.

38. A group of shops in Regent Street seen in the late 1920's, with a Raleigh Service Depot, motor cycle agents in the foreground, then M.B. Brewster's fruit shop, a chemist, then Murdoch, Murdoch and Co, musical instrument dealers, with Arthus Negus and Sons, builders, beyond that.

Regent St, Cambridge

39. Another view of Regent Street, again the work of Ted Mott and taken from the top of a bus as it headed into the town. Ted Mott was a remarkable man who printed a great many postcards from his home during the 1920's. He was born in Markyate, lived first in Chesterton and then at Shelford where he had a fancy goods shop. Usually he cycled around Cambridge and the villages with his plate postcard camera to get the views he wanted. They were then sold at one penny each. He died in 1947.

40. Hills Road Wesleyan Methodist Church stood on the corner of Norwich Street for one hundred years until demolished in 1973. At the time of this photograph in the 1920's the Dorset Temperance Hotel stood on the other corner of Norwich Street. In the group of buildings further along the road with the flagpole was the 'House of Commons' public house.

S 1927   **HILLS ROAD, CAMBRIDGE.**

41. The first of two Edwardian postcards taken for the Kingsway Real Photo Series from nearly the same spot on Hills Road. This view looks towards the City centre along Hills Road and shows the Great Northern Hotel on the right at the entrance to Station Road. The tram lines can be clearly seen in the centre of the road turning up Station Road.

S 1924   **STATION ROAD, CAMBRIDGE**

42. Now the photographer has turned to look down Station Road to the distant railway station. Prominent in the right foreground is Rattee and Kett's, Kett House, now the site of modern offices also named Kett House.

43. Postally used in 1915 this photograph shows the 'Bull Hotel' horse-drawn carriage and an Ortona motor bus waiting with other vehicles outside the Great Eastern Railway Station. The station building was designed by Sancton Wood in the Italian style and opened in 1845.

Mill Road, Cambridge.

44. Just before the railway reached Cambridge, at the census of 1841 there were some 24,453 inhabitants of the city. The railway passing though the east of the city encouraged development near. In the Mill Road area the development was firstly inside the line of the railway in the 1870's and this was followed by the Romsey Town area. At first there was a railway crossing along the Mill Road, but the railway company agreed that should there be the need it would put in a bridge. It became necessary and the bridge can be seen in this Tams' photograph which shows the view looking into Romsey Town around 1900.

45. The ARC Knitting Company was at no. 12 Mill Road around 1907 when this photograph was taken. Above the shop was the office of the Sturbridge Brick Company, the nameplate of the Secretary, Arthur Bayles can be seen on the door at the side of the shop.

Head Quarters of the Cambridge Town Football Club.
George Scott - Proprietor.

46. The Salisbury Commercial Hotel stands on the corner of Tenison Avenue and Wilkin Street. In December 1908 George Scott the proprietor sent this postcard to wish a friend Christmas greetings... 'You will scarcely recognise the man with the short beard but that's your humble servant...' In recent years 'The Salisbury' has been a public house owned by CAMRA – the Campaign for Real Ale.

47. W. Bell had a family butcher's shop at 59 Ross Street on the corner of St. Philip's Road, one of the many small shops that came with the housing development in the Mill Street area in the late Victorian period.

48. The Fitzroy and Burleigh Streets area of the town in the early years of this century had a lively mixture of shops, public houses and residences. This it was considered was where Cambridge's main shopping area away from the College dominated centre would develop. Indeed as this lovely photographic postcard of Fitzroy Street postally used in 1906 shows Laurie and McConnall's department store complete with band stand on the roof rebuilt after their fire of 1903 was already there among the smaller shops. In Burleigh Street was a large branch of the Co-operative Society. After years of controversy and debate over the area which became known as 'The Kite' that development did take place in the early 1980's, not perhaps as was first imagined but with a new covered shopping complex called 'The Grafton Centre'.

49. 'The Forester's' public house selling Bailey's Ales stood on the corner of Burleigh Street. It is photographed here in about 1890 and shows the street before the Co-operative Society built their large branch stores there.

50. Apart from the pencilled word 'Cambridge' on the back of this superb Edwardian photographic postcard of a shop, there was no other clue as to the name of the shop or its position in the town. Quite often, and infuriatingly, this is the case with such photographs that were probably printed in very limited quantities. The shop was eventually identified with the help of the Cambridge Evening News as that of Erasmus Naylor in Norfolk Street. Erasmus Naylor, who stands in the doorway, was the uncle of Richard Naylor who has a grocer's shop at 94 Mill Road, Cambridge today. The site of Erasmus Naylor's shop seen here is now a block of flats.

51. S. Wilson had a small grocery business at 81 High Street, Chesterton. The photograph dates from around 1930.

S 1918   BROOKLANDS AVENUE, CAMBRIDGE

52. Before Brooklands Avenue became associated with various Government offices it was as this postcard, postally used in August 1911, shows a narrow unmade, tree-lined avenue.

The Plant House, Botanic Gardens, Cambridge.

53. The Botanic Gardens in Bateman Street were opened in 1846 on a twenty acre site. In the Kelly's Directory for 1904 the garden is described as 'well arranged and contains an extensive collection of indigenous and foreign plants: in the centre is a piece of ornamental water, and the whole garden is surrounded by trees and shrubs, arranged in such a manner as to afford the most complete facility for reference: the hot houses are spacious, and contain a variety of curious and valuable exotics'. In 1888 and 1891 the plant houses were rebuilt at a cost of over £5,000.

S 1935   LENSFIELD ROAD, CAMBRIDGE

54. Two more cards from the very good Kingsway Real Photo Series. The first is of Lensfield Road looking towards the Catholic Church. The tram lines can be clearly seen down the middle of the road, otherwise the traffic can be described as very light, unlike modern times when the road is a main traffic route.

S 1933   TRUMPINGTON STREET, CAMBRIDGE.

55. An early motor vehicle makes its way between the horse-drawn carts and bicycles along Trumpington Street towards the town centre. The tram lines can be seen in the middle of the road. The trams stopped running in 1914 and while the card probably dates a little before that it was postally used in 1916 by what reads like a soldier passing through: 'Just arrived at Cambridge where I am changing, time 10 o'clock. Have cleaned buttons on train, I leave here 10.30... Plenty of soldiers here.' It was written to his wife in North London.

56. Quite unusual to find the postcard photographer moving so far out of the City centre. But here, around, 1930 Ted Mott is in Grantchester Street. The focus of his attentions is the shop and sub-post office of Mrs. Mercy Mary Cornwell, from which he might anticipate a number of the cards would be sold. As the city spread out, so such small sub-post offices were established providing an easily accessible service to the residents of particular areas. In recent years given the greater mobility of people and post office economies the numbers of such sub-post offices is being reduced all the time.

57. Not far away at Trumpington in 1924 the freedom to travel brought about by the motor car has also brought one of its inherent problems for the postcard photographer to record for all to see. Eventually, and it still hasn't finished, the motor car will destroy more of Cambridge than just the corner of some unfortunate person's house. In 1924 the problems were only just beginning.

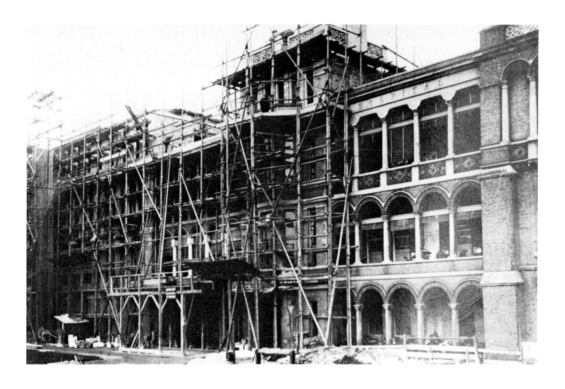

58. Anyone injured in that accident at Trumpington would not have had to go far for hospital treatment. Addenbrooke's Hospital on the Trumpington Street which can be seen through all Rattee and Kett's scaffolding was founded in the eighteenth century following a bequest of some £4,500 by John Addenbrooke, M.D., who died in 1719. The first hospital building was put up in 1740 for the care of 'poor people of any parish or county'. In 1766 an Act of Parliament was passed for making it a general hospital and to be able to obtain the further funds necessary to expand its work. Over the years great sums were raised and many additions and extensions made. Eventually the pressing need for a modern and much enlarged hospital led to work beginning on the new Addenbrooke's Hospital in Hills Road, the first stage of which was opened by the Queen in May 1962. The old Addenbrooke's Hospitally finally closed in 1984.

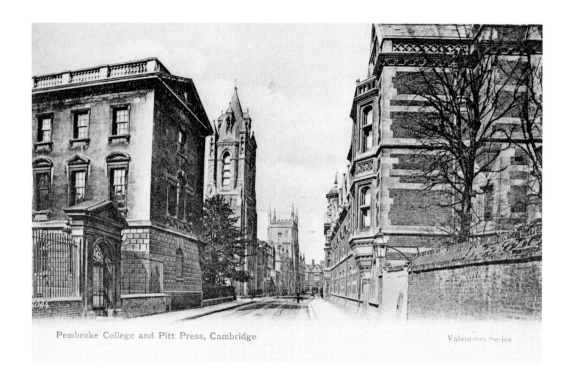

Pembroke College and Pitt Press, Cambridge

Valentines Series

59. The Pitt Press or University Printing Office on the west side of Trumpington Street was chiefly paid for by funds raised to commemorate the statesman, William Pitt. The Marquess of Camden, Chairman of the London Pitt Club, laid the foundation stone in November 1831 and opened the building on 30th April 1833. The Cambridge University Press is the oldest existing Bible publisher and printer in the world. It received its royal printing and publishing warrant in 1534 from Henry VIII. Pembroke College on the right hand side of the view was founded in 1347 by Mary, daughter of Guy de Chastillon, Comte de St. Paul, and widow of Aymer de Valence, 2nd Earl of Pembroke.

KING'S COLLEGE & PARADE, CAMBRIDGE.

60. This classic view of King's College Chapel was sent by Wilfrid to Bert and Bessie at Kettering in July 1904 with the following message: 'Only got to Cambridge last night. Walter repaired my bike before starting. It's about had its day and wants pushing. However, I expect to reach Clacton sometime today.' As can be seen there was a hansom cab rank in Senate House Hill.

CAIUS COLLEGE AND SENATE HOUSE, CAMBRIDGE.

K. m.

61. It is the same cab rank but this time by turning round we have a view of the Senate House on the left and Caius (pronounced Keys) College beyond it. More properly known as Gonville and Caius College it was founded in 1348 but the part seen in this photograph fronting Trinity Street was rebuilt in the years 1868-1870. At the Senate House the degrees are conferred and other public business of the University is carried out. When the University returned Members of Parliament they were elected there with the Vice-Chancellor being the returning officer.

62. Downing Street photographed around 1905. On the left can be seen the Law School and University Museum opened by Edward VII in 1904. Opposite in the foreground at the entrance to Corn Exchange Street was until 1876 Cambridge's first Corn Exchange then H. Liddiard's cycle depot: 'has the best accommodation for housing and cleaning cycles... Unequalled to meet all requirements for cyclists, and all kinds of repairs undertaken'. The University Bicycle Club was also there. Next to Liddiard's was Whitmore and Co, wine merchants and distillery agents. Both buildings have been demolished and Corn Exchange Street is the busy entrance to the Lion Yard multi-story car park.

CAMBRIDGE. THE BACKS.

63. Queens' Road known as 'The Backs' and photographed here in around 1908. Here in one stretch of road the gardens of St. John's, Trinity, Clare, King's, and Queen's straddle the Cam by a series of small bridges.

RIVER FROM SILVER STREET BRIDGE, CAMBRIDGE.

S 1930

64. Silver Street bridge is the dividing line between the more formal college 'Backs' and the more rural grazing land of Laundress Green and Sheep's Green. This is a fine view, again in the Kingsway Real Photo Series, and shows the old cast iron bridge and the Anchor public house, still a popular point for hiring boats. The card was postally used in 1916. A road bridge at this point has been traced back to the fourteenth century. This cast iron bridge was built in 1843. Owing to the heavy traffic it carried and bad design a survey in 1913 showed the need for a new bridge. Repairs were done, however, and the bridge lasted another forty or so years, until a new concrete bridge, clad with portland stone, was opened in 1957.

65. Nearly every College along 'The Backs' it seemed had to have its own bridge over the Cam. Trinity Bridge was designed and built by James Essex in 1764-65 and appropriately has three arches. One of the previous stone bridges was pulled down during the Civil War in 1643 by Cromwellian soldiers in their defence of the town.

66. This is really quite an early photograph of the Jesus Green footbridge. I have seen it dated as early as 1870, but the view was still being used as a postcard in Edwardian times. Before 1836 there was a sluice on the Cam at this point and then that was replaced by locks. The date of this bridge is unknown, possibly 1868, but as can be seen it was at a low level with a High Back over the locks. This photograph from the Chesterton Road side shows the lock keeper's cottage and Jesus Green beyond it.

67. A later photograph which shows the new bridge constructed before the end of the nineteenth century in about 1892 and all at one higher level. The next photograph will give a closer look at the fine Victorian houses on the Chesterton Road that can be seen beyond the bridge.

68. 'Edie' sent this card in 1910 and identified where she lived at 49 Chesterton Road by the common practice of marking the front of the card with an 'x'. These fine town houses look over the Cam towards Jesus Green.

Chesterton Road, Cambridge.

69. Chesterton was a separate parish, a straggling village along the north bank of the River Cam. In 1912 part of the parish of Chesterton was formed into the Cambridge Without civil parish and ward along with part of Cherry Hinton and Grantchester and Trumpington, returning one Alderman and three councillors to the Cambridge Borough Council. In 1922 under the provisions of the Cambridge Corporation Act the civil parishes of Chesterton and Cambridge Without were included in the civil parish of Cambridge. Chesterton Road before the need to cater for the traffic pouring in and out on the A10 in this photograph by William Tams is almost unrecognisable today. On the left is the sub-police station at the corner of Milton Road. The junction with Victoria Avenue is also seen before the development of Mitcham's Corner as it became known after the shop established there.

70. The Spring public house now known as the 'Rob Roy' on Chesterton Road in the late 1920's next to the Tivoli Cinema. The Tivoli was built by Sidney Byron Andrews and opened on 19th March 1925 with a feature film and a London orchestra playing live. The architect was George P. Banyard. The Tivoli closed its doors as a cinema on 19th November 1956 and became a warehouse.

Victoria Ave., Cambridge.

71. The junction of Chesterton Road with Victoria Avenue in the late 1920's with Mitcham's shop beginning to dominate the corner.

72. The row of shops just around the corner from the Victoria Avenue junction with Chesterton Road, photographed by Ted Mott around 1930. At this time Miss Elsie Oxberry kept a hardware shop and post office, next to her was C.T. Green, confectioner and dairyman, then came Freeman, Hardy and Willis' shoe shop, Barker's chemists and Thomas Westrope, watch maker. The manner in which the shop fronts project from the main building suggests they might have been added to cater for the growing population as the new housing estates were developed.

73. The Arbury Road Baptist Church was built in 1930 and shows how Cambridge was spreading northward at the time. No doubt to keep pace with the accelerated growth of the Arbury Area in the 1960's a striking modern extension was built on the right hand front of the existing church and a new entrance arch and foyer were created in 1965.

Humberstone Road, Cambridge.

74. When the De Freville estate in Chesterton came onto the market as building land in the 1880's, it was developed with similar looking villas lining similar looking tree-lined avenues. William Tams photographed Humberstone Road around the turn of the century. This card of Humberstone Road has written on the back: 'This shows our road from the P.O. So you can hardly see our house, it is just where you see the 3 children on the road on the left hand side.' Apart from the sales to local residents at that post office mentioned, it is difficult to imagine this card having a very wide appeal.

Kimberley Rd. Cambridge

75. Kimberley Road like the nearby Pretoria Road in the De Freville area of Chesterton shows the preoccupation with South African affairs at the time they were developed at the end of the nineteenth century. In this Ted Mott photograph taken around 1930 the cars and vans look intrusive compared with the earlier photograph of Humberstone Road. It is, of course, the shape of things to come.

water st Chesterton Cambridge

76. Ted Mott the photographer again around 1930 recording some old cottages in Water Street, Chesterton, with the 'Pike and Eel' public house in the distance. The cottages have subsequently been replaced by some undistinguished housing at Fallowfield. The 'Pike and Eel' had its own ferry across to Stourbridge Common.

The Ferry, Old Chesterton,

77. A lovely photograph by William Tams of the smaller of the two ferries that operated from the 'Green Dragon' public house in Water Street, Chesterton, and Stourbridge Common. This was the ferry for pedestrians while next to it the large Horse Grind Ferry could carry a horse and cart and was much used for ferrying coal over the river. The ferryman for many years was Alf Ford until in 1935 a footbridge was constructed at the spot. The ferries must have been busy when the main annual Cambridge fair was held on Stourbridge Common in the second half of September and the first part of October, but both the ferries and the fair finished in that same year of 1935.

78. The need for a bridge over the Cam at Chesterton was obvious from the number of ferries operating along that stretch of water in the nineteenth century. From a ferry at the 'New Spring' public house over to Jesus Green, there were another eight before the 'Pike and Eel' ferry was reached. The River Cam Bridges Act of 1889 laid down minimum standards for future bridges and the next year the much needed road bridge to link with the A10 traffic was built. It was the iron Victoria Bridge designed by John Webster. Concern over the amount of traffic carried by the bridge eventually led to the building of the Elizabeth Way Bridge in 1971 giving a second road crossing from the north.

79. With all the development in Chesterton the pressure was applied for better pedestrian links with the centre of the town across the Cam instead of the ferries. This postcard was published at the time of the opening of a footbridge link from Pretoria Road across to Midsummer Common on 2nd September 1927. The footbridge replaced the old halfpenny ferry which operated between the Gonville and Caius boatyard and the Fort St. George public house. The ferry operated by Walter Pauley, assisted later by his son, Ernest, sank while not in use shortly before the new footbridge opened.

80. Between Chesterton and Baitsbite Lock the University boat races take place. The May Races which are an inter-college competition are held on the first or second Wednesday in June and on the three following days. They are known as 'The Mays' and because of the narrowness of the river they are bumping races where the boats are started in order of a league table. As soon as the pursuing boat catches the one in front, a bump is recorded and the boats change places in the league table. The Mays have their origin in the rivalry between Trinity and St. John's Colleges which put the first eight oared boats on the river in 1826. Four boats raced in 1827 and from then the number of boats increased rapidly. In 1852 the practice of dividing the boats into divisions was established. The winning boat becomes Head of the River.

81. At the turn of the century huge crowds came to spectate. At Ditton the Rector set up marquees and provided teas in the Ditton Paddock to supplement his income, while on the opposite bank was a small fair. As can be seen from both these photographs spectators took up every vantage point they could from the specially built grandstands to the roofs of carriages and the tops of omnibuses.

The May Races
Cambridge,
The Race Home.

82. Those who went to watch The Mays by boat often indulged in an unofficial race back to Jesus Locks once the last bumping races were over. The river was jammed with all manner of craft and there was considerable risk to life and limb. Harry A Moden, who drew cartoon postcards depicting town and University life in Edwardian times, showed in 'The Race Home' a humorous view of the event, which from some contemporary accounts of the chaos on the river does not seem too exaggerated.

DITTON FERRY
OVERTURNED JUNE 10 05
WHEN THREE PERSONS
WERE DROWNED.

T. T. WING & SON
CHESTERTON
CAMBRIDGE

83. Tragedy did strike after The Mays in 1905 with an accident to the ferry at 'The Plough' at Fen Ditton. Ditton Ferry was known as the 'Red Grind' and James Skinner was the operator at the time with Henry Clayton the conductor. On 10th June 1905, the ferry had made two trips already after the last race. On the third trip with twenty-two passengers already on board, two University men jumped on when it was about three yards out and the ferry lurched over snapping the chain. Three local girls were drowned. The ferry was replaced but eventually removed after another accident following the Lent races of 1961.

84. With rowing such a major College sport it is hardly surprising that boat houses line the northern bank of the River Cam in the area opposite Midsummer Common. There are nineteen of them from the Victorian to the modern. An anonymous photographer during the floods of 1918 shows two of the boathouses. This is Trinity Boat House, which was the first to be privately owned by a College, opened in 1872. It was extensively repaired in 1919 and replaced by a new construction in 1935. Why are the soldiers crowding the balcony? Troops did camp during the First World War on Midsummer Common and with no rowing taking place during the war years some of the boat houses were used by the military. This might have been a temporary use caused by the flooding.

85. The charming late Victorian boat house of Emmanuel College was opened in 1895 and apart from the loss of the balcony looks much the same today. This flood photograph shows the ferry operated by the Dant family for sixty years. David Dant owned the land in the photograph until his death in 1893 when much of it was sold. The Dants continued to live in the cottages seen next to the boathouse. Cutter Ferry Lane ran down to the ferry and there had been a Cutter Inn nearby. In 1927 a footbridge similar to the one near Pretoria Road was built and the days of Dant's ferry were over. The cottages where the Dants lived have also gone but the boathouse and the footbridge, known as the Pye Bridge, are still there with some more modern buildings behind them.

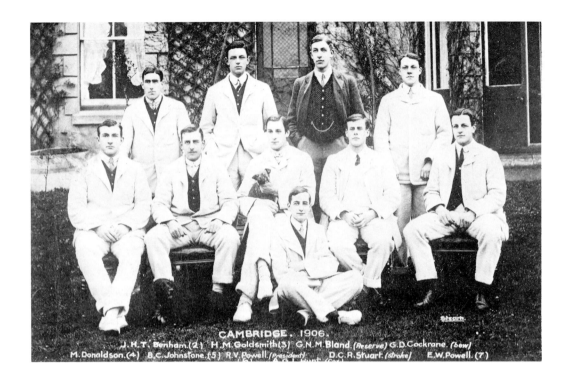

CAMBRIDGE. 1906.

J.H.T. Benham (2) H.M.Goldsmith (3) G.N.M.Bland. (Reserve) G.D.Cochrane. (bow)

M. Donaldson. (4) B.C.Johnstone. (5) R.V.Powell. (President) D.C.R.Stuart. (stroke) E.W.Powell. (7)

86. Many people who have never seen a boathouse on the Cam still follow the fortunes of the Cambridge University eight in their annual challenge race from Putney to Mortlake on the Thames each year with Oxford University. The University Boat Club was established at Cambridge in 1827. The first boat race against Oxford was held at Henley in 1829. In 1836 quite by chance, or rather through the choice of a Mr. Phillips of Christ's, who ran to a nearby shop for a piece of ribbon to distinguish the Cambridge boat and came back with a light blue piece, light blue has been the University colour for all sports. In 1906 the crew seen here were clear winners over Oxford paddling home by 3½ lengths. They were, however, much criticised for their fast but ugly style.

Varsity Crew, 1907. J.H.Priest, Cambridge.

87. Their stroke in 1906 and 1907 was D.C.R. Stuart who gave his name – the 'Duggie Stuart style' – to their effective manner of rowing which did not suit the purists. The 1907 crew of A.B. Close Brooks, bow, J.H.F. Benham, H.M. Goldsmith, J.S. Burn, H.G. Baynes, B.C. Johnstone, E.W. Powell, D.C.R. Stuart and R.F.R.F. Boyle, cox, again won easily by 4½ lengths. On the back of this card it says: 'This snap of the Varsity having an 'easy' has just appeared it is a good one.'

University Boathouses, Cambridge

Valentines Series

88. Before the boathouses on the Cam there were boatbuilding yards in the nineteenth century with such well known names as Winter, Foster, Pocock and Banham. The University and Colleges rented their boathouses from the boatbuilders. In this late nineteenth century photograph the University boathouses were in Foster's boathouses. Note the ferry in the foreground and the pleasure craft moored nearby.

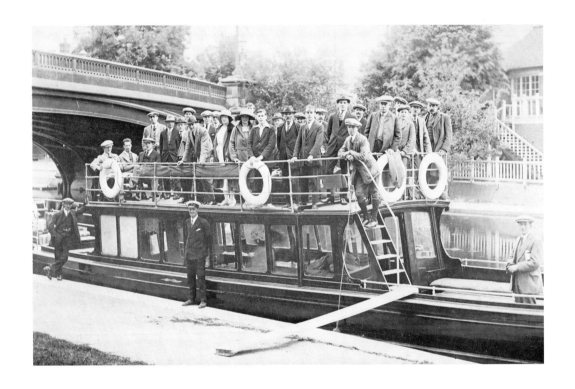

89. For centuries the Cam was used for commerce, as well as rowing. Boating trips for parties as well as small rowing boats were also popular. Victoria Bridge can be seen in the background as a boating party pose, with their smiling captain, for an unknown photographer to record the occasion around 1920. A favourite trip was to Baitsbite lock and there were several popular riverside hostelries like the 'Green Dragon' and the 'Pike and Eel' at Chesterton and 'The Plough' at Fen Ditton on the way.

90. A superb photograph by William Tams of Charley Driver diving at the Sheep's Green swimming station. Charley Driver was custodian, life saver and swimming coach there from 1903 until 1937. He did a dawn to dusk duty, seven days a week and during his career saved ninety lives. Jack Overhill who has swum there every day, summer or winter, for sixty-two years, including his wedding day and his diamond wedding anniversary, when his wife watched him on both occasions, described Charley Driver as 'an amazing man'. For all the talk of river pollution, Charley Driver only had three weeks illness during his period there and Jack Overhill has an even more incredible record.

CAMBRIDGE ON THE GRANTA

43833

91. The Granta is a tributary of the Cam and the Ouse. It rises on the Herts/Essex border and is joined by the Rhee and the Bourn Brook before reaching Cambridge. As the ancient name for Cambridge was Grantabridge, it is claimed that the Cam should really be known as the Granta. Whichever part of the Granta or Cam this is it is an idyllic Edwardian picture of less hurried times.

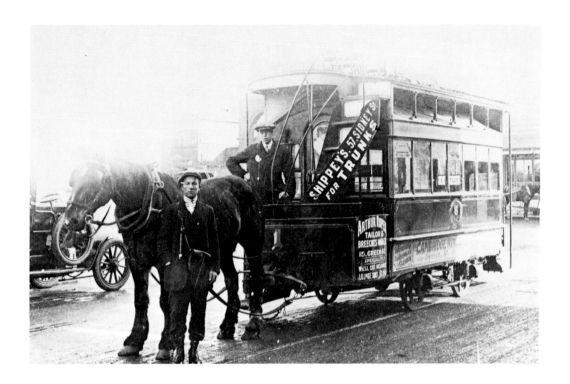

92. Several of the photographs show the tramlines that were once such a feature running through the City centre and out to the railway station. The Cambridge Street Tramways began a regular service in 1880 and the trams continued to run until 1914, although the tram lines remained in some of the streets for several years afterwards. Here one of the horse-drawn trams with its conductor and driver waits outside the railway station.

93. Horse-drawn buses like this were a rival to the horse tram. The Cambridge Omnibus Company began a service in 1896. The side of this bus indicates 'Chesterton, Bridge Street, Market Hill and the Railway Station' as its route. To counter this competition the Tramways Company ran their own horse-drawn buses. The Cambridge Omnibus Company, however, went out of business in 1902.

94. The trams soon, however, had other rivals. On 15th April 1905 two companies began the first motor bus services in the city in competition with each other and the tram company. The Cambridge University and Town Motor Omnibus Company Limited operated a 25 h.p. Straker Squire CE 299 seen here on the Market Hill probably on the first day of service. Their buses were painted light blue and on the first day of operation carried 1,705 passengers between 4.30 p.m. and 9.30 p.m. at a one penny fare. Their rival company was the Cambridge Motor Omnibus Company operating two double-decker Thorneycroft buses.

A BIT OF OLD CAMBRIDGE !

Topical Series—Published by the Cambridge Picture Post Card Co.

95. It was, it seemed, the end of the line for the horse-drawn tram. Frank Keene, the local cartoonist who along with Harry Moden drew for their Cambridge Picture Postcard Company, produced a drawing of a sad and delapidated tram with only one passenger and a sleeping conductor. This card was postally used on 7th July 1905, shortly after the new motor bus service had begun.

CAMBRIDGE
UP TO DATE!

96. Another Frank Keene card from 1905 suggests, however, that all was not entirely satisfactory with the new motor buses. His cartoon creation given the number CE 999 is seen running over a dog, smashing a lamp post and terrifying the passengers. In fact the companies did have a poor safety record and were causing much damage to kerbs, lamp posts and other objects they came into contact with. So much so that in 1906, the next year, both companies had their licences to operate withdrawn.

Topical Series—Published by the Cambridge Picture Post Card Co.

97. Frank Keene was quick to point out the irony of the situation. This card, published in 1906, is black bordered in the style of an 'in memoriam' notice for the Cambridge Motor Omnibus. The horse-drawn tram is full again and bears the slogan – 'A Bit of Old Cambridge – Still Running'.

98. Just over a year later, however, in August 1907, an important figure arrived in the story of Cambridge public transport. He was James Berry Walford and this time it did herald the eventual end for the horse-drawn tram. James Berry Walford began the Ortona Bus Company in Cambridge despite the set backs of the other two companies. The name came from a cruise ship he had seen. The number 1 service was from the railway station where this bus is photographed, via the post office at Petty Cury to the Chesterton terminus. Buses ran every 15 minutes from 8 a.m. to 9.35 p.m. daily except Sundays. The Ortona buses, which had leaf green livery with red wheels and body trim, soon impressed everyone with their service and safety record.

Bus Terminus, Chesterton, Cambridge.

99. In the 1920's the Ortona Company was operating the Leyland G type buses. With rival firms now operating in the city, principally the Burwell and District Motor Services Limited, a new bus station was opened in 1925 at Drummer Street on land taken from the side of Christ's Pieces. On 11th July 1931, about a year after Ted Mott took this photograph of one of the Ortona buses at Chesterton, the company was taken over by the Eastern Counties Omnibus Company based at Norwich. The green of Ortona gave way to the red of Eastern Counties and another local company was now part of a much larger organisation. It was the end of an era.

100. Many of the larger hotels had their own horse-drawn carriages or buses to bring their patrons from the railway station to the hotel. This is the 'Lion Hotel' carriage. The 'Lion Hotel' or earlier known as the 'Red Lion' stood in Petty Cury. It was an eighteenth century coaching inn and in the nineteenth century became one of the only places with a large assembly room, so it featured prominently in town and county life. The large yard behind it, however, became the site for much needed central car parking. In 1965 the 'Lion' closed and was demolished in 1968. The site then provided the major part of the controversial Lion Yard development with shops, library and multi-story car park.

101. Carriers took goods in their horse-drawn carts to and from the city to the surrounding villages and towns. Quite often they had their pick up points at public houses. Fosters Goods and Parcel Express operated in Cambridge in the late nineteenth century. In an 1888 Directory they had premises at 3 Union Street, while in this photograph from around the turn of the century the agent was A. Henderson of 58 Sidney Street where Joshua Taylor had their tailors and outfitters.

102. The milk cart coming round with its churn was a familiar sight on the streets of most towns in the early years of this century. The name on the cart appears to be Wright and the lettering on the side could be Cherry Hinton.

103. In the years before the First World War there was an annual horse and van parade on Midsummer Common on Whit Monday. Prominent in this Starr and Rignall photograph are the vans of Matthew and Son who had a grocery business at 19-21 Trinity Street from 1821 until 1962. As Mr. Bernard Matthew, the last owner of the business, recalls: 'A great deal of work was put into the preparation of horse and vehicle for this parade. No paid overtime! I remember that most of our horses had an array of rosettes on their stall in our stables in Trinity Street... We were all getting motor vans after the war and the horse drivers were having to learn to drive motors. All, except one, of our drivers made it, though all missed their horses.' The vans of Eaden and Lilley can also be seen.

104. Midsummer Common was, and still is, the place for large gatherings and events. After weeks of anxiously waiting for news of the British forces beseiged in Mafeking during the Boer War, the reports that the garrison commanded by Baden-Powell had been relieved in 1900 were greeted by great celebrations. In traditional manner a massive bonfire was built by the town on Midsummer Common. The undergraduates built an unofficial one on the Market Hill using shutters and fences that they tore down. Such escapades by the undergraduates became known as 'Rags'.

105. Both Frank Keene and Harry Moden drew several cards illustrating Rags and Ragging. Such Rags could lead to damage and destruction of property which caused considerable ill-feeling between town and gown. To celebrate Guy Fawkes night on 5th November large crowds would gather and there would be bonfires and fireworks in the centre of the town. In about 1912 Harry Moden drew three cards presumably based on real incidents from the 5th November celebrations: The first seen above is 'The attack on the Tram'.

106. In 1911 a crowd of some 300 undergraduates tried to cross the Jesus Lock Bridge and was held back by five policemen. The third card, not illustrated, shows 'The Station Raid', with milk churns being overturned at the railway station. After the First World War the November Rag activities became associated with raising money for the Earl Haig poppy fund. Hoaxes and good humour replaced the former destructive element. In 1969 February became Rag time instead of November with the activities now aimed at raising money for a variety of charities.

107. The Proctors are responsible for the disciplining of the undergraduates. It is an ancient office and at one time until the nineteenth century they could arrest and imprison prostitutes. The undergraduates in all the Harry Moden cartoons are wearing gowns and indeed all had to do so at night until 1965 and it was the Proctors' role to see they did. In this photograph one of the proctors is seen leaving the University Church of Great St. Mary's, wearing his traditional costume accompanied by his two officers, known as 'Bull Dogs' and they are wearing their formal attire of heavy blue capes ornamented with gilt buttons and tall silk hats. Usually the bull dogs wore black suits and bowler hats. The photograph would appear to date from about 1908.

If I succeed in passing the "General"

Love from Arnold

108. A College bedmaker as seen first through the pen of an anonymous cartoonist. It was a postcard, crudely drawn, but obviously intended to appeal to the undergraduate. Perhaps the cartoonist himself was up at the University.

109. The reality as captured by the camera at the turn of the century. In Victorian times and until the 1930's no unmarried woman could be employed in such a position. One College went as far as to say that applicants had to be 'of horrible appearance'. Known generally as 'Bedders' they cleaned, washed up and made beds for the undergraduates and fellows in the Colleges. Their modern equivalent do the same today.

110. Floods always brought out the cameraman. Here the depth is indicated by those standing up to their thighs in the floodwater. The photograph was of the 1879 floods, unusually a summer flood on the 3rd August, and this particular scene was taken between the Granta Brewery and 'The Jolly Millers'.

111. Floods in August, then why not snow in late April? The Backs with all the trees covered in snow and a thick layer on the road. The date written on the front by the anonymous photographer is Friday 24th April 1908.

112. S.F. Talbot, the Linton photographer, had a high vantage point opposite the Senate House to capture the arrival of King Edward VII in 1904. The King was in Cambridge on 1st March to open the Squire Law Library, Law School, Medical School, Botanical School and Sedgwick Museum.

LA TRIO
POR LA TRIA
CAMBRIDGE
1907.

Photo: J.H. Priest, Cambridge.

113. A major event in Cambridge during the summer of 1907 was the holding of an esperanto congress. 'La Trio por La Tria' shows the three for the third. This was the third esperanto congress and these were three of the organisers. The sender of the card identifies Harold Mudie as the figure in the centre. The Congress was held from 12-17 August 1907. J. Cyprian Rust, the vicar of Soham in Cambridgeshire was a great advocate of such a universal language and he preached at St. Mary's Church in Esperanto.

114. This postcard of the Market Place with flags strung across it bears the message: 'Cambridge is decorated up as there are 1,500 esperantists here learning us their language. Was a grand day yesterday with them. This is where it is held.' The photograph shows the Guildhall, which having been much enlarged and improved in 1862 was eventually demolished in 1936 and the present Guildhall built on the site in 1938-39.

115. Among the stalls on the Market Place for the Congress was this enterprising one selling postcards with a message for all esperantists to read and a notice 'Oni parolas Esperanton tieci', which must mean Esperanto spoken here.

116. In his short jacket and Eton collar, a pupil of the Leys School is about to make a presentation to Sir Henry Campbell-Bannerman, the Prime Minister, who is leaning forward slightly in the centre of the photograph. The occasion was the laying of the foundation stone for the new gymnasium at the school in 1907. The Leys School was established along the Trumpington Road in 1874 by Wesleyan Methodists.

OPENING OF NEW WESLEY CHURCH CAMBRIDGE BY MRS RUNCIMAN OCT.30.1913.

117. This photograph by Scott and Wilkinson of Cambridge records the opening of the new Wesley Church at the corner of King Street and Short Street by Mrs. Runciman on 13th October 1913. The building which could hold a congregation of 700 with the Minister's House and Sunday School cost £20,000. The sender of the card has marked with a cross the Hills Road Minister, the Reverend Lewis.

118. When the Liberal Government's controversial budget of 1909, popularly called 'The People's Budget' as it proposed extra taxation to aid the poorer sections of the community, was rejected by the House of Lords, Mr. Asquith, the Prime Minister, went to the country. The election was held in January 1910. Stanley Buckmaster had been the City's Liberal M.P. since 1906, but at the election his Conservative rival, Mr. Paget, defeated him by 4,667 votes to 4,080. This topical cartoon card by Harry Moden was posted on 2nd February 1910 and shows the varying reactions to Buckmaster's defeat.

119. Despite the comments of the two Great Eastern Railway employees on the former card, Stanley Buckmaster was back in the city sooner than anyone could have anticipated. The Liberals were returned nationally but with a reduced majority and by December the same year there was another general election. Cambridge writer Jack Overhill remembers as an eight-year-old chanting: 'Vote vote vote for Buckmaster, Turn old Paget out of town, For Bucky is the man, And we'll have him if we can, If we only put our shoulder to the wheel.' The result, however, was unchanged. Paget defeated Buckmaster by 343 votes, a slightly larger margin than Buckmaster's original 1906 majority, so this time Stanley Buckmaster did leave Cambridge.

120. Two typical Cambridge police constables have little difficulty in controlling the crowd awaiting the Proclamation of King George V at Shire Hall on 10th May 1910.

121. The Cambridge Salvation Army Band photographed at tea in July 1912. Cambridgeshire has always had a strong banding tradition and in modern times the Cambridge Co-op band is establishing a formidable reputation in national contests. The photograph is by the well known Cambridge and Ely firm of Starr and Rignall.

122. Roller skating or 'rinking' was a popular Edwardian pastime. The Cambridge Roller Skaters were described as 'a vigorous society'. The message on the card posted 19th January 1910 reads: 'Here is a picture of the new Cambridge rink.' This was almost certainly the Rendezvous in Magrath Avenue which was opened around this time, although there were other rinks. In 1919 the Rendezvous became the Rendezvous Cinema but was destroyed by fire in 1931. It was rebuilt the next year and became The Rex Cinema in 1938, which closed in 1972. The building was demolished in 1979.

123. Gonville Rovers Football Club photographed in 1907 when they were competitors in the Cambridge Thursday League. Thursday was half day closing in Cambridge, so a Thursday football league gave young shop assistants the chance of a competitive game of football. The Thursday League began in September 1903 with many of the games being played on Parker's Piece. The first clubs in the league were Beehives, C.E.Y.M.S., Fitzroy Early Closers, Harston Nomads, Lilleys, Linton Granta, Old Perseans and Post Office.

124. 'The last of the wooden spoons (one of 3) Cambridge 1909' is pencilled on the back of this card. C.L. Holthouse of John's carries the huge spoon. According to Enid Porter in 'Cambridgeshire Customs and Folklore': *From about the year 1824 until 1909 it was the custom to give to the man whose name appeared last on the list of Junior Optimes a large wooden spoon, bearing his name and the arms of his College, which was lowered by cords from the Senate House gallery as he knelt before the Vice-Chancellor. The man himself acquired the title of The Spoon or Wooden Spoon.*

Mock Funeral, Cambridge, May 18ᵗʰ 1911.

125. Another University custom which died out later in the 1930's was the Mock Funeral for an undergraduate who was sent down for some misdemeanour. It was a custom which became popular in the late nineteenth century. The 'corpse' accompanied by various mock clergymen and raucous mourners would be taken to the railway station in a lively procession. A card published by Priest records a Mock funeral on 18th May 1911 along Regent Street. At the Station he would be put in the guard's van where the mourners would 'knock nails' in his coffin by beating on the van with broom sticks.

126. An intriguing photograph of some of the pupils of St. Giles Infant School demonstrating with varying degrees of enthusiasm the delights of Boots Malt Extract with Cod Liver Oil. Children were regularly dosed with such things at this time to supplement their poor diet. St. Giles Infant School was in Albion Row, just off Castle Street. In Edwardian times headmistress Miss Jane Shead had some 170 pupils under her charge. For some years now the old school has been a milk depot.

127. There has obviously been some vigorous brushing of hair before these boys in their knickerbocker suits and various collar styles faced the camera for the standard group photograph. St. Luke's Boys School in Victoria Road was built in 1881 and enlarged in 1898 for 365 children. The postcard would appear to date from about 1906, but there is no other information with it. No one has helpfully written all the pupils names on the back and nearly eighty years on, who remembers them all now?

128. The string orchestra of the Perse High School for Girls photographed by Mason and Co. in about 1920. Miss Evans, the music teacher, is photographed with her pupils, but Mrs. Hackforth who started the orchestra in 1919 refused to come before the camera. Miss Jean Robson, who is the sailor-suited little girl with the violin second from the left in the front, and her sister, similarly attired but with a cello, are among the players. The photograph was taken in a temporary hall building erected in 1916. The school, the sister school of the seventeenth century Perse Grammar School for Boys, was begun in Panton House in Union Road in 1873.

129. The days when the gym slip reigned supreme. July 1920 and the young ladies of the hockey team of the Perse High School for girls face the camera of Stearn and Sons of Cambridge for the annual team photographs. Someone has pencilled the names on the back, but possibly some years afterwards because there is some doubt, signified by a ? as to the identity of some of the girls. Back row: ?Marjory Hopkins, Ba Willis, Kathleen Theobald, ?Winifred Strangeways and Kathleen Farr. Sitting: Elizabeth Glover, Lynette La Touche, Gwen French, Miss Reed and ?Marjory Hopkins. In front: Alys Narborough and ?Dorothy Strangeways.

130. On 4th August 1914 the Company Commander of the 1st Cambridgeshire Regiment received a telegram: *Mobilize, first day of mobilization August 5th*. The country was at war with Germany. Recruiting began at once. In Cambridge on 9th August the hall of Pembroke College was taken over by the Red Cross. The Hall of Corpus Christi was the headquarters of a special war committee. The Cambridge Companies of the 1st Battallion the Cambridgeshire Regiment enlisted many officers and men from the Cambridge University Officer Training Corps. The colours were marched under escort to Great St. Mary's Church and handed over for safekeeping. Soldiers were billeted in schools and houses all over Cambridge and on Midsummer Common the VIth Battalion were under canvas as this photograph shows.

131. An ammunition column of the 4th Battery, 2nd Welsh Brigade, Glamorganshire, photographed in Cambridge during the First World War. The building is the Drummer Street frontage of Emmanuel College. During 1914 and 1915 the 53rd Welsh (Territorial) Division was billeted in the City.

132. Different College buildings were used by the military during the First World War. On the back of this card is written: 'St. Catherine's College, Cambridge, 1915.'

133. When the men were called to arms during the First World War the women took over many of the jobs more usually done by the men. Here two are photographed in 1917 on Cambridge Corporation road sweeping duties.

1st Eastern General Hospital, T. Cambridge.

Copyright Photograph by J. Palmer Clarke, Cambridge.

134. The First World War took many local men to France to fight. Special hospitals were established to tend to the wounded who were sent back to England. In September 1914 the First Eastern General Hospital was established in Nevile's Court in Trinity College. Soon the hospital moved to a larger site where the University Library is now. The hospital was a series of low, long huts as can be seen from the photograph by J. Palmer Clarke of Cambridge.

135. On 3rd August 1916 King George V visited the Hospital unit. He is photographed here being greeted by Colonel J. Griffith, the officer commanding the hospital.

136. Harry Moden had stopped drawing his cartoon cards before the war, but the victory celebrations caused him to draw one more to give an impression of the scenes in Cambridge when it was known that the war was over.

CAMBRIDGESHIRE WAR MEMORIAL.
UNVEILED BY H.R.H. THE DUKE OF YORK. K.G.   3/7/22

137. A much more solemn occasion on 3rd July 1922 when his Royal Highness, the Duke of York, unveiled Cambridge's war memorial. A young soldier with the victor's laurel wreath draped around his rifle strides along. The memorial was placed at the junction of Hills Road with Station Road, so his glance to the right looks down towards the railway station from which many young men departed, some never to return.

138. Thurston's gondolas photographed at Chesterton Fair in the 1920's. Cambridge still continues its historic fair tradition with an annual fair on Midsummer Common. Thurston's of Cambridge are still a leading name in the world of touring fairs.

139. Originally built in 1814 by William Wilkins senior, to replace an earlier theatre, this was the interior of the Barnwell Theatre or the Theatre Royal, Barnwell. It was part of the Wilkins' theatrical circuit in East Anglia. In 1878, however, it became a mission hall. In 1926 the building on the Newmarket Road was renovated and reopened as the Festival Theatre by Terence Gray, assisted by Harold Ridge and Norman Marshall. The stage was adapted as an open stage by the removal of the proscenium and proscenium arch doors. The three tiered late Georgian auditorium was kept virtually the same. The Festival Theatre was only active until 1934 but during those eight years it built up a considerable reputation. With the opening of the Arts Theatre in 1936 the Festival Theatre became the scenery store for the Arts and is still used as a scenery store and workshop.

140. The New Theatre and the Cambridge Daily News offices in St. Andrew's Street in about 1929. The New Theatre was built by W.B. Redfern in 1896 and presented all the leading London companies. Faced with the competition from the cinema it became a Theatre-Cinema in the 1930's. It was television, however, that brought its closure. That was on 17th March 1956 when 'Cabaret de Paris', one of the many similar saucy touring shows that were around at the time had been playing. The building was demolished in 1960. The 'Cambridge Daily News' was founded by William Farrow Taylor in 1888, so it first appeared around the time of some of the earlier photographs in this book. In 1962 the paper moved to new offices on the Newmarket Road, where, as the 'Cambridge Evening News' now, it continues to tell the story of Cambridge that these photographs have been a small part.